Homegrown Leadership

by

Marty Fitzgerald

Table of Contents

Why Leadership? 1

Meetings 8

   Observing 9

   Leading 15

   Driving from the Backseat 22

Office Politics 31

   Know the Players 31

   For the Good of the Company 34

   Political Equity 36

Intrinsic vs. Extrinsic Power 40

   Extrinsic Power 41

   Intrinsic Power 42

   The Relationship of Power 43

Mentoring 48

Productivity 56

   Setting Expectations 58

   Give Them the "What" 61

   Listen to the "How" 65

   Allow Them to Succeed 69

   Reward Success 76

Levels of Leadership 82

Managing Up 90

Prioritization 99

Organizational Priorities 100

Team Priorities 102

Individual Priorities 105

Decision Making 111

Hiring 119

Firing 130

Conclusion 140

A very special thank you to my sister, Kelly Ise, for putting in the time and efforts to make the final version much more polished than the original.

Why Leadership?

I was once asked what I needed to be happy in a job as a leader. As this was later in my career, and I had many years of leading both large and small teams under my belt, I was able to answer very succinctly and definitively with these two points:

1. I need to be able to provide value
2. I need to be able to take care of my team

If a company will not allow me and my team to do work that is directly adding value to the organization, then my work has no purpose, and we are equivocally wasting each other's time. We all need to make money. (Well, most people do.) We spend a lot of our lives trying to make it so we can pay our bills, give our kids a better life, buy things, go on vacation, eventually retire, and a trillion other reasons. Having to get up every day and fight the traffic to and from work to go to a meaningless job where you add no perceivable value is a very empty way to spend decades of your life. In addition, if I am not allowed to lead my team in the manner I deem appropriate in order to add value to the organization, then they don't want a leader, they want a manager. And I am a leader.

At some point in our careers, many of us are faced with a dilemma which can best be described as "to do" or "to lead." We spend years building expertise in a given discipline, and then we reach a point at which we have to decide whether we are willing to forego our continued pursuit of expertise in that discipline in order to lead people. My experience throughout my journey has taught me that it is very difficult, if not impossible, to do both well.

My internal process went something like this: "If I can produce X as an individual contributor, and what I value is being able to produce, then how much more could I produce if I had a team of several people who could each produce *at least* X individually? Wouldn't my contribution of value increase exponentially as a leader as long as I were able to lead effectively?" Seeking the answer to that question led me on a 25-year journey through large corporations, non-profit organizations, start-up companies, and industry-leading businesses, all the while honing my skills as a leader and learning from the mistakes I made along the way.

I have been infatuated with the idea of leadership since I was very young. My father was a police officer and led a tactical squad, and I admired the way his men respected him. In sports, I paid attention to the techniques and mannerisms of my coaches. I noticed how the athletes responded to the different coaching styles; how some coaches got the very best out of individuals and, of equal importance, which ones couldn't. After high school I studied the leadership skills of drill sergeants in basic training for the U.S. Army and NCOs who might have been asked to lead young soldiers into battle. Doing so allowed me to distinguish, beyond instinct, the ones I would proudly walk into a firefight with from the ones I wouldn't so confidently follow. There were also all the bosses, from my first job to my last. I experienced the difference between the boss who everyone greets in the morning and the one who everyone just watches first to gauge the mood because that is the indicator for how the day will go, the ones that build people up, and the ones that tear them down, the ones that take all of the blame and give all the credit to their team, and the ones that do the opposite. I pinpointed the traits in all of these leaders that I liked and worked very hard to emulate them. The traits that I didn't like, I worked equally hard to avoid. My style of leadership evolved over many, many years. It is a passion of mine that I cultivate continuously.

This book came about from mentoring several new managers that were working on growing into effective leaders. I would mentor up to a half dozen young leaders at a time, but I always challenged them to bring topics to me about which they were interested in learning more. I didn't have the time or inclination to try to figure out what they wanted to learn. We would spend as much time on a topic as they wanted. I would answer all of the questions I could and give examples of things I had done well and even those not so well. If they could learn from my mistakes and avoid them in their own careers to become a better leader than I was, then in my opinion, I was doing what I should be doing as a mentor. What I began to notice was that most of them had questions on similar topics. I had to start taking notes to remember what I had covered and with whom. Consequently, those notes allowed me to create a menu of topics from which they could choose if they had a hard time selecting a specific topic themselves.

I am guessing you have been able to ascertain this by now, but before we go on I want to state clearly that this book has nothing to do with becoming a good manager. There is a distinct difference in managing and leading. If your desire is to become a good manager, then this is not the material for you. This book is about leadership.

Notes

Meetings

There are several types of meetings. Most of them are unproductive and usually just lead to more meetings. I don't really care about types of meetings as there is a ton of literature out there on that topic. What I do care about is your role in any given meeting. It will be one of three: Observing, Leading, or Driving from the Back Seat. Each role is important, and each has its place. If you execute your role well, then you have done what you can to make a meeting as productive as possible. Unfortunately, you cannot control how other people execute their roles in meetings. Too often, the people who should be observing are trying to lead or are jockeying for some political position not relevant to the objective of the meeting.

Observing

I will lay out how you should spend most of your time in meetings, especially if you are not leading. In any given hour-long meeting where you are a participant, spend your time this way:

First 30 minutes:

- Do not talk unless you are asked a question directly. This is not to say you should be rude or antisocial, but you need to listen and observe. Many times, meetings are called with no specific agenda or objective. While I personally do not agree with this, it happens quite frequently, so spend the first 30 minutes gaining understanding.

- Understand the objective of the meeting. This is where the type of meeting may come into play. Is it just to disseminate information? Is there some action required by you or your team? Is this meeting setting the stage for something bigger down the road or a strategic political move?

- Note who is doing the speaking. Is it the leader, as it typically should be, unless the leader called the meeting to gather specific information? Pay attention to the tone of the people doing the speaking. Are they defensive? If so, are they being attacked? By whom if they are? Is someone attacking or blaming?

- Study the body language of the participants. Who is waiting for their turn to speak? Who is just speaking over others because what they have to say is

more important than what anyone else
has to say? Who is engaged and who is
not? Specifically note the behaviors of the
ranking officer in the room if it is not you.
Are they paying attention? If they are,
then understand why it is important to
them and make sure you are anticipating
questions you might be asked.

- Be aware of political posturing. It can
  show up in many ways, but watch for
  people selling an idea that is outside what
  seems to be the objective of the meeting
  or defending an idea that may only
  marginally be connected.

- Write down what the objective is once
  you understand it along with any
  questions or thoughts you have had in the
  first 30 minutes.

Next 20 Minutes:

- Listen for any of your questions to be answered. Note the answer if it is. Do not ask a question that has already been answered unless you need some clarification. This just proves you weren't paying attention. Ideally, all of your questions will be answered in these 20 minutes, but that won't always happen.

- Given that you have understood the objective of the meeting within the first 30 minutes, discern whether a path to meeting that objective is becoming clear. Keep in mind that there may be more than one path to meet the objective of the meeting.

- Pay attention to the people who are speaking. Do they see a path to meet the objective? If so, are they following it? Many people will get a spur of the moment idea and think out loud in the meeting only to realize that the idea will not meet the objective. Don't be one of those people unless it is a meeting specifically for brainstorming.

- Formulate a path to meet the objective in your mind. It doesn't have to be a wholly original thought either, you can piggyback off of a path that someone else has already started. Do not let having your own idea blind you to other possible paths that could be just as effective. It is just as valuable to support a good idea as it is to come up with one of your own.

Last 10 Minutes

- Think before you talk. Let me say that again: THINK...BEFORE...YOU...TALK!!! If you are unsure of what words are going to come out of your mouth when you open it, then keep it closed.

- Restate the objective as you understand it. Do this in the form of a question or as in seeking clarification if the objective was not explicitly stated at some point. This may be helpful to you as well as to other participants in the meeting. Omit this step if the leader of the meeting has done it.

- Ask any questions that you had written down that have not yet been addressed in the meeting. Make sure they are still relevant to the objective of the meeting before you ask. And, again, do not ask a question that has already been answered unless you need clarification.

- Offer the path you formulated to meet the objective if one has not emerged thus far in the meeting. You can also offer support for a path that has been identified, but only if what you have to say adds value. If all you are going to do is to restate what has already been said, don't.

- Repeat out loud any action items and/or deadlines if no one else does. Again, do this in a clarifying manner if you are not leading the meeting or were not specifically assigned as the scribe for the meeting.

Every word that you say that is not in line with the objective of the meeting waters down any words that do add value. If the ratio tips too far the wrong way over enough time, no one will listen to anything you have to say. Think Before You Talk!

Leading

The most important thing to remember about leading meetings is that you need to know what you want the outcome to be before you call the meeting. It may be as simple as a status meeting at which you only need to convey information, the desired outcome being that the audience walks away with the knowledge that you needed them to have. On the other hand, it may be as complex as trying to get a group of executives to come to a decision. In such a case, the objective may be to lead them to a very specific decision that you want them to make, or it may be just a decision so your team can move forward. The number of variables and scenarios is endless, but there are some fundamental steps you can take to help you get to the outcome you desire. Bear in mind that you are not always going to get the outcome you want, and you need to be able to operate with whatever outcome you get. The following steps, however, will increase the odds in your favor of getting your desired outcome.

- Define the desired outcome, then set the agenda to achieve that outcome. The order in which you deliver information is important. Think of it as taking the attendees on a journey to get them where you want them to be. Set your agenda in a logical path to get them to that place. Say, for example, you need to call a meeting to get approval to buy a piece of equipment for your team. A logical path would be to state the reason that you need the equipment or the problem that it fixes for the organization, e.g. efficiency, cost savings, or revenue production. You could then explain how the equipment meets the need or solves the problem, state the financials, show the return to the company in hard numbers, follow up with any ancillary benefits, then ask for approval on the purchase. You would not, in this case, want to spend 20 minutes of an hour-long meeting going into a detailed history of the piece of equipment or explaining how you and the CEO of the company had science class together in high school.

- Always send the objective and the agenda in advance. Do not ask people to give up time in their day without them knowing what they are giving it up for. If everyone is trying to add as much value as they can to the organization, then you need to extend the courtesy of allowing them to decide if your request for their time is more valuable to the organization than something else they could be doing. You should expect the same courtesy. Remember that the objective and the desired outcome may or may not be one in the same. Always state the objective of the meeting. The desired outcome is for you and those assisting you to know. In our equipment purchase example, the objective of the meeting is to get a decision on the purchase of the equipment. The desired outcome is for the decision to be approving the purchase.

- Invite the fewest number of people possible. This one can be a little tricky. There is a tendency for everyone to want to be "in the know", so people get offended when they are left out of a meeting they wanted to be in. If your objective is to get to a decision, then remember that the more people you invite, the more opinions there will be. If the decision is about resources, i.e. time, money, space, and/or people, then you need to be aware of any attendees who might be adversely affected by a decision in your favor. You must also consider whether omitting a particular colleague might result in your team losing access to something essential. There is definitely a delicate balance between getting as few of the right people to your meeting as possible without damaging your ability to navigate going forward.

- Know your audience. People receive information differently. You may be a brilliant engineer who can explain the technical intricacies of every piece of equipment in an entire factory, but if you are meeting with executives who do not even know how to turn a single piece of that equipment on, then your technical jargon will be lost on them. If you want to achieve your desired outcome, make sure the journey you take your attendees on makes sense to them, not just to you. Otherwise, they will have no idea where they are when they get there.

- Observe your audience while you are speaking. Are they paying attention, and are they engaged? Are they bored? Are they understanding what you are saying? If your audience is not with you, then you may need to adjust on the fly. Although doing so is not recommended, it is sometimes necessary. One way to effectively gauge your audience is to ask someone a very easy question that you know they know how to answer and will answer in a manner that supports your desired outcome. It could be something simple, like asking someone to explain something you just said when you know they already know the answer. When leading people on a journey, a good leader looks back every now and then to see if everyone is still following. If you could have gotten to the desired outcome yourself, you would not have had to call a meeting.

- Be efficient and respectful of your attendees' time. Don't schedule an hour for something you can cover in 15 minutes, but don't feel bad about ending a 30-minute meeting after 20 minutes if you have met your objective. You do not have to use the entire scheduled time, but never take more than the time you scheduled. If you are deadlocked near the end of the meeting, then schedule another meeting.

- Repeat the outcome at the end of the meeting. It is uncanny the number of times people will sit in the exact same meeting and hear different things. List any action items and/or deadlines along with the person to whom they are assigned. Follow up the meeting with documentation of these items to all attendees and impacted/interested parties.

Driving from the Backseat

The concept of driving from the back seat is fairly simplistic. Executing it effectively can be extremely difficult. Conceptually, all you have to do is everything that you would do if you were leading the meeting, but before the meeting happens, and then get the person who is leading the meeting to verbalize your objective and drive toward your desired outcome in the meeting and think it was all their idea. This one takes some practice.

- Just as with leading a meeting, you need to know the outcome you want from the meeting. Said outcome may or may not be directly in line with the objective of the meeting if there is one stated, but it cannot be too far off, otherwise this technique won't work. An example of misaligned desired outcomes would be if the leader is trying to get resources assigned to a project, while you are trying to get new computers for your team. In this scenario, not only are you not in the back seat, you aren't even in the same vehicle. If, however, what you are trying to achieve is that your team isn't overcommitted and given unrealistic deadlines, then you have a shot at steering things the way you would like them to go.
- Ask for the objective at the beginning of the meeting if one was not offered prior to the meeting. If one was given, then ask

a clarifying question about it. This will take some diplomacy. You cannot challenge the leader and put them on the defensive. If they feel like you are saying their objective is wrong, then you've lost your chance at leading them.

- If the objective as stated in the meeting is not in line with what you had planned for prior to the meeting, then offer a suggestion and ask for agreement. For instance, if the stated objective is to assign resources to a project, you might suggest amending it to assign resources to the project that ensure the best chance of success without incurring overtime costs. Doing so puts you in the position of assisting the leader, especially if the leader is in charge of the project. If you can get agreement on this restated objective, you have protected your team and given them a great opportunity to succeed without working them to death to meet a deadline. You have also helped add value to the organization by giving the project a chance to succeed, as any project that costs three times more than was budgeted for will not be considered a success.

- Know the audience. If the leader is strong willed and very political, you will have a hard time "driving from the backseat". If you understand the stance of other attendees prior to going into the meeting, then you can use that to your advantage. If, for instance, you know that one of your colleagues has a team that is stretched thin, then that could be helpful for you.

- Having a "partner in crime" is not a bad idea here. If you have someone who will support your restated objective, it will be more difficult for the leader to avoid accepting it. It will also keep you from looking like you are just going head to head in a power struggle with the leader.

Rather, you will be regarded as a team member looking to do what is best for the team and the organization. A word of caution: use this strategy wisely and sparingly lest people think you are plotting against them for your own gain. Such an assumption will sink you quickly.

- As always, observe the attendees. You will be able to tell how the information you offer is received. Watch body language to see how they are engaged, and whether they are paying attention. If you find yourself on an island in the meeting, you should probably abort your cause and try another way. If you have some support, then continue on, but tread lightly.

- Ask leading questions toward your desired outcome. Doing so is how you get them to think it is their idea. The words will come out of their mouth first. Use phrases such as, "Have you given any thought to…?" or "What do you think it would look like if we…?" Then, help them develop the idea that you had already thought of before the meeting.

- Pull people back to the objective if they start to go down a rabbit hole. This takes some tact as well. Forming it as a question like this may work, "Can you please help me understand how that helps us get to what we agreed was our objective? I may be missing something."
- Repeat outcomes, action items, and deadlines if no one else does, or ask the leader to refresh your memory on what they are. Ask that the documentation on the meeting be sent out to the group.

So, you might be asking yourself why so much concentration on meetings in a leadership book is necessary. There are several reasons, one of which has already been stated; you will spend a lot of your time in meetings, so you need to do your part to make them as productive as you can. The second is that meetings are where a lot of the political games are played, e.g., people jockeying for position, or trying to increase their own clout or power. You need to pay attention to what is going on and who is doing what so you can understand the playing field. If you understand the playing field, you will know how to move and when to defend so you can take care of your team and add value to the organization. The third one is that you have to remember that you are always representing your team and the work that they do. Meetings are your chance to communicate to your peers and superior officers the success of your team, the challenges they have overcome, and to boost the reputation of individual team members as well as the team overall. The last is related to the third. Obviously, the team being able to produce quality work, on time, and within budget is primary to their reputation. However, the manner in which you conduct yourself in addition to how you are regarded by others in the organization will set the tone for how your team is viewed within the organization. Meetings provide you the stage, when appropriate, from which you can be your team's cheerleader or their defender. Often it is the presentation you make on this stage that helps get more work assigned to your team so that they can continue to add value.

Notes

Office Politics

If I had to choose a single word as advice on office politics, it would simply be "DON'T." Unfortunately, that doesn't really work so these are a few strategies that I have found to be helpful in navigating these tumultuous waters.

Know the Players

It is helpful to understand the people you are dealing with and what motivates them. Using the observation techniques we discussed in the chapter on meetings is a great tool in this regard. Take note of mannerisms, how often people talk, how they respond, especially if they respond emotionally. Watch their body language and where they choose to sit in meetings. Do they always sit directly across from or right next to the highest ranking person in the room? Are they always in a position to be seen and heard at all times? Do they have side conversations while others are speaking? Do they command attention or beg for it? Are they the type of person who always finds fault with any idea that isn't theirs, or do they climb in the boat and start paddling the same direction as someone with a good idea?

You will start to get a feel for what a particular colleague values, which will give you insight into what political games they will engage in, what they are hoping to gain by engaging in the games, and how they might go about navigating a particular situation to get what they want. Some people want power and/or the titles that come with it. Some want respect. Some need to be heard. Others need to be "in the know." It is not a bad idea at all to schedule one-on-one meetings with peers and superiors to help you get to know them and their teams. Be specific and intentional in these meetings. Don't just schedule time to chat, but don't ignore the benefit of building relationships either. Once you have a feel for what people value, you can start to understand which people can be valuable to you in a given situation. It can also help you to watch out for which people may make moves that could be detrimental to your team. You will undoubtedly need allies. Know the difference between who will always be in your corner, who will never be in your corner, who will use you to get what they want, and who you can partner with to get what you need for your team, even if they are not a full-time ally.

Understanding the players in the game will help you tailor messaging to each one that will play in your favor. It will also help you be prepared for what they might say so you can tailor your response. Ego plays a big role in office politics, so pay attention to what people seem to get passionate about.

For the Good of the Company

Know that office politics are emotionally charged and become personal more often than they should, and strive to diffuse the emotional energy. There is a huge difference in saying "I think...", "I feel...", or "I want..." and "In the best interest of the company..." while backing it up with sound data. Understand that you will not always win. That's okay. Sometimes the emotion or ego becomes more important than what is best for the company. Be aware there may be games at play that you may not be privy to, e.g. someone trying to sacrifice a pawn to take a bishop. Having trust in your leaders is essential to job satisfaction. If you do not have it, it may be time to start looking for a position elsewhere.

Even if you are met with a "because I said so" emotionally charged order, continuing to conduct yourself and being perceived by others as having the best interest of the organization in mind will eventually pay dividends. If everyone acted in the best interest of the organization, made decisions based on facts rather than feelings, and were able to set egos aside when someone else presented a better course of action for the company, then office politics wouldn't exist. The reality of the situation is that we are human beings dealing with human beings, and emotions are a part of the package; the good, the bad, and the ugly.

Political Equity

Political equity is a bit like a savings account. You make small deposits over a period of time, and you can see it grow. You can make calculated withdrawals every now and then for the right reasons, but one foolhardy decision can drain the whole account at once. Deposits into your political equity account come in the form of adding value. People knowing of your successes or witnessing them is helpful. Bringing a project to a successful completion, offering a solution to a problem, even having one of your team members compliment your leadership to another leader all deposit equity into your account. You may spend some when you need to hire a new member for your team, when you miss a budget item, or when a project runs over. The easiest way to drain your account is to have an overly emotional, negative response at the wrong time in front of the wrong audience. It is important to have a gauge on your political equity as well as on that of those with whom you engage. Build it daily and spend it wisely.

I do not believe that I have ever encountered a person who admitted that they enjoyed office politics, yet there are clearly some individuals that thrive on the drama. One of the things that I believe is backwards in organizations is for most people the focus is on the individual first. How do I get promoted? How do I get a raise? How do I get a better position or a better title? Focusing on, having pride of, and showing loyalty to one's own team comes second. All of which puts the organization as a whole last. It looks like this: individual > team > company. The reality is we could all accomplish so much more if this were reversed: company > team > individual. A good leader will understand that the better the company does, the more able he/she is to take care of the team, which in turn, leads to individual opportunity and growth. The professional political gamer will find themselves on the path to having the biggest title and the most power in a company that is struggling to stay afloat.

Notes

Intrinsic vs. Extrinsic Power

The power that you have goes a long way in determining what you can control and what you can influence. Typically, the more power you have, the bigger each of these circles. Your circle of control is normally smaller than your circle of influence. What you control often times comes with extrinsic power. What you are able to influence, both inside and beyond your circle of control, is often dictated by the extent of your intrinsic power.

Extrinsic Power

The simpler of the two to explain is extrinsic power, so let's start there. Extrinsic power comes with title and position. In the U.S. Army, a captain has control over a company of soldiers, so his or her extrinsic power is over a couple of officers and several dozen soldiers. A colonel, however, may command a battalion, giving him or her extrinsic power over multiple captains and several hundred soldiers. The higher the "rank", the more extrinsic power you have, and typically the larger the circle of control. Bear in mind that this power or control does not necessarily correlate with the number of people under your purview. It could be processes, decision-making authority, fiscal responsibility, or a number of other things that give you power.

For instance, in a given organization, a vice president may have a team of 100 people performing a function, such as IT for the business. In contrast, another vice president in the same organization performing a different function, say finance by way of example, may only have 20 people under him or her, but hold the funding for the entire organization. Both vice presidents hold a significant amount of extrinsic power with different sized teams and different resources under their direct control.

Intrinsic Power

Intrinsic power has more to do with your ability to get people to do what you need them to do without the aid of position or title. It is your ability to get people to do the things you need them to because they want to, not because they have to in order to keep their job. It is someone fulfilling your request rather than having to follow your order.

Intrinsic power, like respect, is earned and built over time. It has a lot to do with how you are perceived by others on your team and in your organization. Intrinsic power is more about influence than control. As your intrinsic power grows, so does your ability to influence a greater number of resources.

So how do you grow your intrinsic power? Well, basically, by doing the things that your kindergarten teacher taught you: work hard, treat others like you want to be treated, turn your work in on time, pay attention, listen more than you speak, do your best, be nice… you get the idea.

The Relationship of Power

So now that we've looked at the different kinds of power, it is important to understand the relationship between the two. Intrinsic power is something you should always be striving to increase regardless of your position in an organization. It has been my experience that growing your intrinsic power will often times lead to an opportunity for extrinsic power or increased extrinsic power. It is extremely important to pay attention to how you are perceived in the organization. Do not make the mistake of only caring how you are perceived by your peers and those above you. They may be the ones that promote you, but it's the people below you that will make you successful. Bear in mind that you can have intrinsic power without extrinsic power. When the boss walks out of the room and there is a task to be done, who do people look to, who do they listen to, who do they ask questions to, who takes the lead and gets things done while bringing the rest of the team along with them? It should be you, and people should be coming to you because you earned their trust and respect and they know that you will help them all be successful. The person who tries to lead to impress the boss, or just outright takes the lead because they're overly ambitious or are just a bossy person, does not have intrinsic power. They are just annoying.

Conversely, you can have extrinsic power without intrinsic power. Don't be one of these people. These are the people who will do anything they can to climb the ladder to get the position they want, and they don't care who they step on to get there. These are the people who everyone hates working for. They may be smart, well-spoken, polished, and highly political, or they may be that vice president who is perceived as incompetent and everyone wonders how they rose to that position. In either case, their success will be limited because their people will only do what this "leader" orders them to do.

Ideally, from a leadership perspective, you want as much extrinsic power as your experience warrants and more intrinsic power than extrinsic power. In this situation, your extrinsic power is justified by your experience, so your intrinsic power will not suffer for it external to your own team. Internal to your team, if you can lean on your intrinsic power so your team performs because they want to rather than because they have to, your chances of succeeding increase exponentially. Of course, you will need your extrinsic power occasionally with your team, but if used correctly, it will actually increase your intrinsic power with them. And one last time in closing: ALWAYS PAY ATTENTION TO HOW YOU ARE PERCEIVED!

Notes

Mentoring

This is an area of my leadership growth that I wish someone had forced me into earlier in my career. I will admit that I had a hard time asking for help. That was a foolish mistake on my part. I sought mentors later in my career, but I really could have used the help and advice of a trusted mentor many times as a young leader. My advice to you is to get at least two mentors as early in your career as possible. You don't need to be in a leadership position to have a mentor. Don't wait. Having someone to help you navigate difficult situations that they have probably seen before will only accelerate your growth and keep you from stepping in the same potholes that may have slowed them down at one point.

The reason that I recommend having at least two mentors is a matter of perspective. It is important to have at least one who is internal to your organization and at least one who is external. Both can assist you when wrestling with a decision or an issue, give advice on navigating politics, handling personnel, or motivating your team, or even just be a sounding board while you work through something out loud for yourself.

For an internal mentor, I would suggest someone who is not in your direct chain of command. This is not a hard and fast rule, but rather just a recommendation. Having one person who is not in your chain of command but is in your discipline and one who has responsibility outside of your discipline is ideal if possible. If you have fairly narrow vertical, then this may prove difficult, but if you are under an executive that has multiple teams, choose a mentor who is not on your team and then one who falls under a different executive.

Every team has its own dynamic, its own politics, and even its own personality. Having a mentor who is on a different team within your discipline can help you with very specific things within that vertical. They can help you understand how you and your team are viewed within the larger team. They will have a more in-depth understanding of the personalities on the team and can help navigate political waters within the team and organization.

Having a mentor who is internal to your organization but outside of your discipline offers another perspective on you and your team within the organization. Personally, I preferred to have someone as a mentor who was an internal customer to my team. It helped me to make sure we were providing the best service we could to the people in our company who were counting on us to deliver. I could get honest feedback on performance and personalities, as well as advice on how to improve and serve them better. It also gave me a chance to see the organization through a different lens and understand the challenges that people faced outside of my own little world. Broadening my own perspective and understanding of what the organization looked like through different lenses helped immensely in making sense of and navigating office politics.

An external mentor can help you with general situations. They won't necessarily know specific personalities, but they will probably know personality types and can offer up experiences where they have had to work through similar situations or with similar personalities. They can also help get you out of the mindset of your company if you are stuck in something. Sometimes we get so caught up in how we do things at an organization that we can't see another way because we are too close to it. An external mentor will not have that bias and can help you step back and see the forest when you can't see it because all of the trees are in your way.

Some organizations have formal mentoring programs, which is great, but don't wait for that. Take the initiative and just ask. The worst they can do is say no, although it has been my experience that most good leaders will gladly mentor someone who is eager if they have the time to do so. If you are going to ask someone for their time, make sure you use it wisely and productively. They are not going to have time to meet with you once a month for an hour just to chat. Have specific topics you want to discuss. Send them the topic in advance, but not too far in advance; a day or two is plenty. If you have a sensitive situation to discuss, then let them know, but be discreet about it when you send your topics. If they give you good advice, and you apply it, then report back to them that you did, and what the results were. I always appreciated knowing what worked and what didn't when I gave advice. It helped me become a better mentor.

One last concept to consider here; you can learn something from everyone you meet. Every encounter, every meeting, every discussion is an opportunity to learn. Take it. You may have a two-minute hallway conversation with the CEO and learn more in that two minutes than you will for the rest of the day. You may ride up the elevator with the mailman and learn something about how to deliver efficiently that you never even considered. Conversely, you may also learn what not to do. You may sit in a meeting for an hour and still have no idea why you were in there or what the point of the meeting was. You just learned from the leader of that meeting how not to conduct a meeting. Opportunities are all around you, so pay attention. Do not dismiss anyone. Everyone is better than you at something, and that something may just contain an answer that you've been searching for. Don't miss out on it because you weren't paying attention or were too arrogant to take a moment to learn.

Notes

Productivity

We have already established that being able to add value to an organization is paramount to success for you as a leader, for your team, and ultimately for the organization as a whole. In order to add value, invariably your team will need to produce something. It could be something completely intangible, such as ideas, or something very concrete, such as a product to be sold. Your team could be directly responsible for the lifeblood of the organization, or it may perform a support function. It is vital for you as a leader to understand the role of your team and how it adds value to the organization. It is equally important that you stay focused, and keep your team focused, on that role. Too many "leaders" try to expand their empires within an organization by duplicating in their own teams a function that the organization has charged to another team. This is unproductive and inefficient. Do not do this. As you and your team consistently and efficiently succeed in adding value, your circle of control will increase. So, this begs the question of how you get a team to deliver effectively, efficiently, and consistently. The formula that I have found to work for me is as follows:

- Set Expectations
- Give them the "What"
- Listen to the "How"
- Allow them to Succeed
- Reward Success

Setting Expectations

Most people want to succeed. Most people will work extremely hard to achieve success. All leaders want their teams to succeed, but not all leaders actually articulate to their teams what success consists of. Do not assume that your team knows what you want unless you specifically tell them what it is, they actually understand it, and can accurately say it back to you. Only then have you adequately set expectations.

As a leader you need to give thought to what expectations you have for your team. Some will be imposed by your team's role in the organization. Some will need to come from you. It is your responsibility to make sure that every member of your team understands these expectations very well and either meets or exceeds them. Some expectations will be general to the team and will always stand, and others may be specific to a project or function that needs to be performed.

General expectations may be around the quality of work that you expect of them. Obviously, there are times when mistakes are more costly and less tolerable than others. However, you want to be careful not to tighten the screws so tightly that people are afraid to fail, because in many situations failing is a good way to learn. I would rather take a few steps in the wrong direction and be able to correct once I know I'm wrong than to be too afraid to move at all.

Another general expectation may be around not missing a deadline that has been committed to. Still another may be that all team members will respect each other. You can't make them like each other, but you can set the expectation that they will treat each other with respect.

One expectation that I have found to be important is making sure they know you expect them to be honest with you. If something is falling behind or is not working, then they need to know that you expect them to be upfront with you. If you set this expectation, then you cannot crucify them for telling you something has gone awry. You need to help them correct it and may need to defend them to your superiors to allow them time to correct it. If something does go other than according to plan, and it will at some point, as the leader, it is your fault. If you have a team member who is consistently not meeting expectations, well, that will be handled in another chapter. Bear in mind that whatever general expectations you set for your team, you must also adhere to. If you expect them all to be at work at 8:00 a.m., and you consistently show up at 8:30 a.m., then not only are you a bad leader, you're a hypocrite, too.

Whether the expectation is specific to a project or general in nature, it doesn't do anyone any good if it is only in your head. You must articulate it to the team so that they understand it. If they do not meet an expectation that you never articulated or that they did not understand, then that is your fault, not theirs. Be specific and consistent with your expectations.

Give Them the "What"

In order for your team to successfully produce something that adds value to the organization, you, as the leader, need to tell them what that is. Personally, I preferred to tell my team what value it added, or why it was important enough to command our time and attention if it wasn't blatantly obvious. It is always helpful for motivation if you know what the value of your efforts are. There may be times when you are not allowed to share the completeness of the value, but I was always a fan of sharing the value when I could.

The "what" may come from several different places. It may need to come from your own head, especially if you are building a team from the ground up and creating a new function in the organization. It could be dictated to you by your superiors. It could be something that came from someone on your team. Do not discount ideas of how the work might be done more efficiently or effectively when they come from the people actually doing the work.

I had a job once where I had to configure and install a computer system for our customers. I was a team of one. The average install time was six months, and the success rate was only about 60% before I started. I spent a few months learning how it all worked and, after a little time, was able to get the install time down to six weeks. However, I was faced with a large backlog of clients, and I could really only work on one at a time. I came up with an idea of how to make things go more quickly and smoothly, but I needed a programmer and several months to make it work. My boss gave me what I asked for and put all installations on hold for eight months so I could get the project completed. It was a leap of faith, but the product was failing and could not keep up with demand. At the end of the redesign, I asked for one additional person to help me do the installs since there were almost 30 by then. Again, he granted my request. I taught my teammate the streamlined implementation process, and together we erased the entire backlog in less than 12 months. After that I always encouraged ideas from members of the team and granted many of them the same opportunity I was afforded.

If the "what" comes from you or one of your team members, then you need to be able to explain clearly to your leadership the value that it brings to the organization. In these situations, I would always ask myself if I were spending my own money to pay for this work, whether or not it would it be worth it to me. If my answer was yes, then I could usually make a good argument for spending company resources on it. If it was no, then it usually didn't go further than that. I would sometimes ask that question to the person who presented the idea. Sometimes they could explain to me a value that I hadn't considered, but sometimes they couldn't. Either way it was a good exercise for them in presenting an idea and justification for committing resources to it. Even if the idea didn't get approved, they were heard and had a better idea of how to get something approved for the next time. Sometimes people wanted to work on things because they thought it would be fun, which was great, but cost always had to be considered. If the cost of a project was more than the value it might have added to the organization, then they had to find some other way to have fun.

When explaining the "what" to your team, be as specific as you can. Take the time to figure out what you know about what you are trying to produce and what you don't know. There may be a discovery process that you need them to go through before things are clearly defined. That's okay. Define for them the questions that need to be answered in order to define more clearly the "what" and listen to any questions they may have. Make sure you and your team are on the same page regarding the "what" before moving on to the "how." Many times people want to start building the house before they even know what the house is supposed to look like. That never works…ever.

Listen to the "How"

This is extremely difficult for some leaders to do, especially new leaders who were very good in their chosen discipline. Once you have made the decision to lead instead of "do," you have to let the people you lead do the doing. You have to let go of solutioning for them. Like I said before, it is nearly impossible to do both well. Even if you have what you are trying to produce halfway built in your head, keep it to yourself unless the team needs help, then give them a gentle nudge in the right direction.

If you dictate the "how" instead of listening to it, you back yourself into a corner. You will stunt the creativity of your team and kill their motivation. They will become robots that are just carrying out your orders, and at that point you will have effectively become a manager rather than a leader. You will find yourself having to manage work and design solutions. You will have no way to grow your people, and you become stuck in your position because all of the productivity is dependent upon you.

I had a boss once tell me that a good answer today is better than a perfect answer tomorrow. Don't get caught up in your "how" being the "right" way to do it or the "only" way to do something. All you need is "a" way to do it. There are a million reasons why something won't work. All you need is one reason that it will. Keep your mind open to the ideas of your team. You can use your experience and your expertise in your discipline to see if their idea is going to run into roadblocks or if there are holes in it, but if it has merit and is likely to succeed, then encourage it. I guarantee you that someone will work harder to make their "how" successful than they will to make your "how" successful. No one likes to be wrong. Remember that even if you were to send them down the path of your "how," they don't think exactly like you do. They aren't going to make all of the same decisions you would throughout the process. They will get lost on your road trying to do what it is that you wanted rather than forging their own path towards a successful solution. Their energies are wasted trying to make you happy rather than adding value. That is a leadership mistake.

A word of caution here. The farther away from the "how" that you are, the more you need to be sure that the progress updates you are receiving are accurate. No one wants to tell the boss that things aren't working or that they are behind. I've seen people give glowing status reports to the eleventh hour, and then all of a sudden everything is off track, and deadlines will not be met. This scenario does not end well for anyone.

That being said, don't sweat the small stuff. I was once in charge of a project that was almost a year long. We knew we had a hard deadline at the end. The team was new, the technology was new, and what we needed to produce was extremely difficult. We missed every milestone along the way - every single one, but I kept telling my bosses that we would make it. I could see how the team was growing, coming together, and getting smarter with what they needed to accomplish. I was giving accurate reports on our progress. I did not sugarcoat anything. The team put in some long weeks in the last month, but we made our date. The team had grown into a very cohesive unit. They believed in themselves and what they were doing. They were not going to allow themselves to fail. And in the end, they were all experts in the technology that none of them had ever seen in the beginning. After that, there wasn't anything they couldn't do.

It's your job as the leader to understand what things are important and what things are not. If you push on the things that aren't important, you will wear out your team, and they won't have anything left for the things that are important. They will know when you have their backs on the small stuff and will work all that much harder on the big stuff. So, don't worry about the small stuff.

Allow Them to Succeed

I know this sounds a bit absurd, but you would be surprised at how often teams are not allowed to do what an executive or a company asks of them. I came across a saying by Konstantin Josef Jirecek once early in my career while working on something that was ridiculously impossible to begin with, had crazy deadlines, and insufficient resources to even be remotely successful. It went like this:

> "We, the unwilling, led by the unknowing, have been doing so much with so little for so long that we are now capable of doing anything with nothing."

It is something I never forgot. If your team is going to be productive and add value to the organization, they are going to need three things from you: a sufficient amount of time, the right tools to complete the job, and most importantly your support.

Let's start with time. I will start out by saying that I absolutely despise arbitrary deadlines. Some people seem to be obsessed with having a date by which something is going to be completed before the work is even clearly defined. I never gave dates unless I was ordered to. If someone asked me for one, I would just tell them no, even when they told me they wouldn't hold me to it. That is an outright lie, so don't fall for it. Once a date is verbalized, it might as well be written in stone because you will be held to that date. I also rarely dictated dates to my teams unless there was a hard deadline that had a good reason behind it. I would define the "what", listen to the "how", and then let them tell me how long it would take. Obviously, I would have to be careful about people padding the dates, so I would challenge them. Only then would I communicate a date when asked, but I always gave my team a little cushion. It also allowed me to hold my teams accountable to the timeline because they were the ones who told me that they could produce within that timeframe.

One thing I've learned about organizations is that most of them seem to have the attention span of a toddler in church. Priorities are going to shift, and sometimes there may be very good reasons for them to be shifting, but not always. If your team is charged with producing something that is going to take six months to complete, and two months later they are given a higher priority task that needs to be completed in one month, they no longer have sufficient time to be successful at producing the first ask. This is where they will need your support. You will need to be able to communicate very clearly to all interested parties that the timeline has shifted. If you do not communicate this and reset the expectation, then your team will be perceived as having failed when they do not complete the first task in the six-month timeframe. You need to protect them from shifting priorities as much as possible. It is disheartening and unproductive for your team to start a body of work and get deep into it, but then not be allowed to finish.

While it can potentially be done, it is extremely difficult to pound a nail in with a screwdriver. If you are going to ask your team to pound nails in, then you need to make sure they have hammers to pound them in with. Of course, you will need to be mindful of things like the budget and people asking for toys just because they think they would be cool to have for the job. They may need a hammer to pound the nails in, but they don't need a new pickup truck to haul the hammer and nails around in. Keep the cost of the tool proportional to the value your final product will bring to the organization. If the company will never get more value than the cost of the tool, the responsible thing to do is to make your superiors aware of this.

As far as support goes, in addition to guarding against shifting priorities and arbitrary deadlines, they will also need you to manage the stress, defend them when they have a misstep, remove roadblocks, and help them when they get stuck. There are going to be times when you have to drive your teams hard to get things done. Make sure you know how much pressure they can take so that you know how intensely you can push them. If you overdo it, they will burn out, and your productivity will take a nosedive. Give them a break when they need it. It was not uncommon for me to tell someone to just take the rest of the day off if they had been hitting it too hard for too long. It was never not appreciated. Even if you are going to miss a small, unimportant deadline, they will appreciate being taken care of, and they will remember that when it comes to the big ones.

No one is perfect. Your teams are going to miss something at some point. Take the heat for it and keep it off of them. Very rarely was I bothered by a mistake. Mistakes happen. There are very few things that can't be fixed, and more often than not a person will feel extremely bad for messing up. Don't make it worse by punishing them. Get them the help they need to correct it. Communicate what you need to, and how it is going to be corrected to those who need to know and go about your business. What I was not okay with was a mistake being repeated. I would take the heat for a mistake that my team made and not come down on them, but if I had to take the heat for the same mistake a second time, then they were going to hear about it. My expectation of it never happening again would be crystal clear, and they would have to lay out for me the very specific steps they were going to be taking to make sure that it didn't happen again.

Roadblocks are going to present themselves, but they may not always be apparent to you. Be clear with your team that they need to let you know if anything is getting in the way of them completing their work. Then when they do let you know, make sure you take care of it. Just like when they get stuck, take care of it. They may not be able to reach an agreement as a team on how to proceed. Get them together, understand their debate as well as the pros and cons, make a decision on how to proceed, and unstick them. They may just be at a dead end or think they don't have permission to make a decision. Again, pull them together, listen to them explain where they are, and give them the permission they need. More often than not they will figure it out while they are explaining it to you. If not, then give them some guidance or get them some help as quickly as you can so they can keep moving.

Reward Success

I specifically titled this section Reward Success because I was terrible at celebrating. Getting everyone together in a conference room to eat cookies and cake just wasn't my cup of tea. That being said, I was at least smart enough to know that some people thoroughly enjoyed that, so I usually had at least one person on my team that enjoyed hosting or organizing celebrations. I had a boss one time who realized he was not perceived as being very approachable, so he had several leaders directly under him who were very personable. He counted on them to makes sure the teams were taken care of. Knowing your weaknesses and augmenting them with the talents of other people on the team is an important part of your own self-awareness. You will make your team stronger and more cohesive by allowing others to step up and perform a role that they enjoy and are skilled at.

Being aware of my own inadequacy at celebrating also made me mindful that not all people felt rewarded in the same way. Money was important to some people so being able to give them a gift card or a spot bonus was always a good thing for them. When giving monetary rewards, though, be mindful that the amount befits the work being rewarded. If you give someone a $50 gift card for a huge project that took nine months to complete, you are probably just going to insult them. On the other hand, if you give someone $500 for completing something trivial, you just set a precedent and an expectation that you will not be able to uphold.

While financial rewards are usually well received when they are on target, some people actually prefer time. Telling someone to take the rest of the day off on a Friday afternoon or to just not come in on Monday because they have been doing a great job and you appreciate all that they have done goes a really long way. Many times I found that people would thank me for recognizing their efforts and continue working. Sometimes I would have to actually tell them to go home because they wouldn't go. That's when you can tell that you have people working because they want to, have pride in what they do, and are not just completing tasks to get a paycheck.

Recognition is also a great reward. You can simply take a moment to stop and talk to someone who has been doing well and let them know that they are doing well. You can announce their accomplishments in a meeting, as well. If you do this, then make sure you only recognize a small number of people. If you are trying to sing the praises of twenty individuals all at once, then you just watered down that praise for every one of them. My boss one time announced a success one of my teams had in an executive meeting where I was present. The success was largely due to one individual on the team. After the meeting the CEO took a moment to congratulate me on the success, and I gave all of the credit to the woman who actually made it happen. Later that week he made a point to go up to the woman and congratulate her on the success and thank her for what she had done. She, in turn, told him that she was only able to do it because of me and gave the credit back to me. My CEO told that story in the next executive meeting as an example of good leadership. I had been unaware of his conversation with her. The perception of me, her, and the whole team was boosted by that one little story.

Other rewards come in the form of raises and promotions, but those happen too infrequently to be adequate or sufficient. Not to downplay their importance by any means, thank you is important to say.As a good friend of mine used to say, "Thank you is nice to hear, but it won't feed my dog." Make sure you take care of the people who need it when the time for raises and promotions comes. Handling this appropriately can be a delicate matter and could be covered in its own chapter. Suffice it to say for now that if you don't financially take care of the people who are producing for you, eventually they will go find someone who will. No one wants to feel undervalued.

Rewards are all about letting people know they are appreciated, that their hard work and dedication in producing for the company has brought value, and it is value that has not gone unnoticed or unappreciated. It takes very little time to tell someone they are doing well. It takes very little time to tell someone else that someone is doing well. In doing so, you may even be rewarded yourself.

Notes

Levels of Leadership

This may seem like a ridiculous topic to put in a leadership book because anyone who has spent a month in any given organization could probably tell you the management structure, at least at a macro level: manager, director, assistant vice president, vice president, C-Level executives, etc. Titles might differ by industry, but the idea remains relatively intact. One possibly superfluous thing to note is that titles are not always indicative of a person's power, experience, or ability. I once left a corporate job in a $2 billion company as an assistant vice president in charge of all applications with over 50 people on seven different teams in three different states across the country to become a chief operating officer in a start-up company of 14 total employees. I had a bigger title, but a much smaller team. Interestingly enough, the level of responsibility was more difficult to compare. In the large organization, if I didn't do a good job, I could get demoted or fired, but in the small company, if I didn't do a good job, the entire company could go under, leaving us all unemployed. All fourteen of us had our roles, and we all knew we had to do them well in order to survive. The point being, titles are just titles, don't get too caught up in them.

What I really want to discuss in this chapter is perspective and how your view of the world you operate in changes with the levels of leadership. Allow me to demonstrate this with a relatively well-known mathematical formula, namely the Quadratic Equation.

$$x = \frac{-b \pm \sqrt{b^2 - 4ac}}{2a}$$

In this equation there are three variables: "a", "b", and "c" where each one is combined and/or manipulated in a given way to ultimately solve for X, giving you the solution to the equation.

As a manager you may be responsible for "c"; defining it, figuring it out, producing it, or solving for it. You don't really necessarily have to know or care how "a" affects "c" or "b". Your mission and focus is "c", and that is the value that you, as a manager, bring to the organization.

As a director, you may be responsible for "a". Now, not only do you have to understand that "a" will be multiplied by 4 in the numerator and by 2 in the denominator, but you also have to care about what "c" is. It is also important to understand that "c" only impacts your "a" in the numerator and not the denominator. So when you are making decisions on how to make the best "a" for your company you have to keep all of these things in mind so that you don't neglect any of them and are also making sure that your manager has what he or she needs to produce "c".

As a vice president, you may be responsible for "b". Now you are no longer dealing with simple multiplication in figuring out "b". You have to consider that the square root could be positive or negative and that you have to subtract your director's work from yours before you take the square root, subtract that answer from your "b", and then divide your director's work from that, all the while making sure that your director has what is required to produce "a", and the manager has what is needed to produce "c".

Finally, as a C-Level executive, you are responsible for "X", the final product or solution. You have to make sure that all of your teams have what they need to produce their own products. You have to know how they all come together, and you have to make sure they understand their piece of the overall equation.

So when the manager is quick to judge the director because from the manager's point of view all that is needed is just this one little thing so that "c" can be produced, and the director is an idiot for not quickly approving the resource or money that the manager may require, it is quite possible that the director is being extremely responsible in considering how to produce "a", and that there is a priority and a complexity to it that the manager does not understand or appreciate. So, before you judge the decisions and actions of those who have a larger perspective of the world in which you operate, make sure you consider that there may be extremely important factors that you are unaware of in your relatively smaller operating world.

In order to lead well at any level, you need to understand what part of the equation you are responsible for and make sure you are considering all relevant factors for the best possible outcome. This, once again, is the value that your team, or teams, brings to the organization. This is of utmost importance. Secondarily though, it is extremely helpful if you have a solid understanding of the world in which the next level in your chain of command is operating. It will help you produce your part better and may help your supervisor produce better, which puts you in a good position to increase your extrinsic power and increase your span of control. Just make sure you have someone on your existing team who is ready to step in and take your place so you can move. We will explore this further in the next chapter, Managing Up. Keep in mind, it can be helpful to have an understanding beyond the immediate

next level in your chain of command, but
spending too much time trying to get into the
details of an operating world too far removed
from you can get you into trouble and distract
you from what you need to produce.

Notes

Managing Up

Now that you have an appreciation for the fact that your headaches are different from the headaches of the people who are on higher rungs of the proverbial ladder, you can start to learn how to use this knowledge to provide value at your level more efficiently and effectively. This, as we have already established, is beneficial to your career and the growth of members of your team, both collectively and individually. If you have done your job well as a leader and grown your people effectively, then opportunities that come your way to you as an individual create openings and opportunities to team members that you have coached to be ready for such opportunities.

Everyone reports to someone. Even the CEO has to answer to the board of directors, who, in turn, has a responsibility to the shareholders, so on and so forth. Just because you are the big boss doesn't mean you get to do whatever you want. Even if you are the one solving for "X", rest assured there will be multiple parties interested in "X" being bigger or coming more quickly or costing less money or making more money or any combination of these and other criteria.

Moving up in an organization is a natural ambition for any aspiring leader. Knowing how to throttle back your ambition so as not to outpace your skills is a valuable thing. Once you reach a certain level, it is highly advantageous to have a few laps around the pool under your belt before moving up. Ambition is great and can get you there, but experience and wisdom are what will keep you there. It's very difficult to build or maintain political equity when you move to a deeper pool that may have sharks in it that you are unaware of.

That being said, we want to focus on the things that will get you ready to move to the next level, and managing up is one of those things. Using our example from before, let's say you are responsible for "c", and your boss is responsible for "a". There are a few things that you can do to make it easier for you to produce "c" and for your boss to produce "a". The first thing is that you need to understand "c" very well. If your boss has not defined the "what" of "c" for you, then ask. And continue to ask until you have a crystal clear understanding of the "what" of "c". Once you understand the "what" of "c", then figure out the "how" of "c", and then tell your boss what the "how" is so that your boss understands very clearly the tools you need to produce "c". Communicate honestly on your progress in producing "c", and let your boss know what he or she needs to know so that they have the information to defend or support your team at levels that you don't participate. And then deliver.

If you've been paying attention, then this should sound very familiar. And the answer to your question is, yes, you can manage up in a very similar fashion to leading your team. Your boss needs you to produce something so he or she can do their job. If you can take care of "c" for your boss, then your boss can focus on "a" knowing that "c" is in good hands. This builds political equity for you and your boss and increases your intrinsic power at the same time.

If you can do this much for your boss while adding your defined value for the organization, then you are in a pretty elite leadership group and are already outpacing most managers in the corporate world today. If you want to take it to the next level, then continue reading. This is how you climb.

Once you have "c" running like a well-oiled machine, then start paying attention to "a". What is the bigger picture? What is the world like that your boss must operate in? How does "c" impact "a", and how can you help "c" make "a" easier to produce? This will require some tact and diplomacy depending on your boss's style, but if your boss is a good leader, he or she should be grooming at least one replacement. And you want to be one of those being groomed given that your experience warrants moving to the next level.

Don't be afraid to express your interest and offer ideas on the "how" if you have them. DO NOT distract from "c" to do this and make sure you observe first so you have a decent understanding of "a" before offering anything. DO NOT offer this in a public setting. Explain what you have observed in a one-on-one meeting with your boss and ask questions. There are more than likely forces at play that you are not able to see. BUT if you demonstrate an interest and understanding of "a", your boss may offer information that will help increase your understanding. Don't be offended if your suggestion is not taken. Take any information offered and continue to build your understanding of "a". Remember, you are here to add value to the organization, not boost your own ego.

Don't be afraid to collaborate with your peers to help make "a" easier to produce. While you might be responsible for "c", one of your peers might have a significant responsibility in producing "a". If you work together, you can both make your boss's job easier. Then, not only have you demonstrated a greater understanding of the larger process while producing "c", but you have proven that you can work with others to produce something greater than either of you could produce alone. In short, be the team member on your boss's team that you want on your team.

One last thing, know what makes your boss tick - what it is that is important to him or her. I once had a VP who was very financially focused. He taught me a tremendous amount about budgeting and managing to that budget. It was a large organization, and his time was in great demand. I was tasked with putting together the financials for a very large software implementation and was having trouble getting the proposed cost to fit the budget. His day was booked solid with meetings, but I had a deadline and no way to meet it without his input. I printed out a spreadsheet that illustrated a multi-million dollar disparity and asked his assistant to place it on his chair. He saw the spreadsheet between meetings and cleared an hour for me so we could work the numbers into what we needed them to be. If I had sent him an email or tried a hallway conversation on his way to a meeting, it would not have worked. He was a numbers guy, and seeing the numbers made it real enough for him to adjust his schedule. So, pay attention to what makes your boss tick and pull that lever only when you need to.

Notes

Prioritization

Prioritization is something that I wrestled with throughout my entire career, and I expect that most leaders do. The way I see it, there are three categories of priorities that you must be dealing with at any given time. The largest scale is priority as it is dictated by the organization, the second is the priorities for your team, and the third is priorities for individuals on your team. Each of these levels comes with their own challenges and complexities. Let's look at organizational priorities first.

Organizational Priorities

At many levels of leadership, organizational priorities can be the most frustrating because you have the least amount of control over what they are or when they change. Even at the highest levels, you may have to shift priorities based on market pressures, competition, a large client being signed, board direction, or a number of other factors that may come into play at any given time.

As I stated before, many organizations have the attention span of a toddler in church. I have witnessed several start-up companies fail because they chased revenue rather than staying focused on their core business. It's easy to get distracted by money, especially as a young company on a shoestring budget, and then wake up one day and really have no idea what it is that your once-very-focused little company even does anymore. I have also witnessed large organizations spend millions of dollars on what initially was a very good idea, but then couldn't stay focused on the end game long enough for the return on the investment to materialize, so they changed priorities and never saw a dime of return on their multi-million dollar spend. So, if you do find yourself in a position to be setting or influencing organizational priorities, make sure you are staying true to the core values of your organization with your decisions, that you truly understand the opportunity cost of shifting priorities, and that you are not just putting down one shiny object to pick up the next one that caught your eye. It happens all the time.

If, like most leaders, you are on the receiving end of the organizational priorities, the first and foremost thing that you need to do is GET ON BOARD. That's not to say that you can't or won't be frustrated, or that you have to agree or like the priority that was set or changed. BUT your team must never see that you are not on board. Remember that you are there to add value to the organization. It is a job, and they are paying you to do it. If you feel the need to express your frustration or need some clarity on why a priority was set or changed, then you do this behind a closed door, respectfully, with your boss. You take what your boss tells you, and you communicate the priority to your team as the best thing for the organization, then you lead your team into executing to achieve that priority.

Team Priorities

As a leader you will undoubtedly be juggling many things all the time, and you will have to decide how to take care of all of them. There can be a fair amount of stress involved in trying to keep all of the balls in the air at the same time. There will also be many times when it is impossible. There will either not be enough money, resources, or hours in the day to get everything done no matter how hard you work or how well you lead. The trick is to understand which balls are rubber, and which ones are glass. If the rubber ones hit the ground, they will bounce, but if a glass ball hits the ground, it will shatter, and you will have a mess to clean up. The hardest part is determining which balls are which. I wish I could give you a perfect formula for figuring this out, but I can't. Time, experience, and having to clean up a few messes will help you as you grow in your leadership positions. I can tell you that if you stay true to your focus of adding value to the organization, and you have good, sound reasons for making the decisions that you do, the collateral damage will be less if you make an error. Communication is key.

If you are faced with making decisions around conflicting priorities, do not be afraid to ask for help, but you need to go about it in a specific way. If you just go to your boss, and you are flustered and just say you don't know what to do, you just spent political equity and decreased your intrinsic power. Plus, it gives the appearance that you are unable to handle the position you are in.

If you need help, then outline the problem. List the pros and cons of each alternative. Be honest. Take the data to your boss in an unemotional capacity and seek advice. In approaching it this way, you have provided your boss with a solid foundation for supporting the decision whether your boss makes it or allows you to. If you drop a glass ball that your boss knows is in jeopardy and has supported your decision, and there is no other alternative, then you are in the best bad position you can be in. If, on the other hand, you do not communicate and make your boss aware of the impending mess, and your boss is surprised by the catastrophe, then you are in one of the worst bad positions. So, make sure you communicate.

I can tell you that I have never gotten in trouble for taking care of clients. If I had to let something drop because I needed to take care of a high-priority need for a client, no boss ever told me that was the wrong decision, even if I had to make it unilaterally in the spur of the moment. This is one of those skills that comes with time and practice, so give yourself a little grace if you make a mistake. Just make sure you learn from it and adjust course for the future.

Individual Priorities

The stress of priorities exists at all levels of an organization. Whether you are leading leaders or individual contributors, you need to be aware of the stress that you are imposing upon them. We will assume for the sake of this section that your team will communicate honestly with you and that you are aware of all of the work that they are being asked to perform. There are several cases where an executive or other leader may walk up to an individual contributor and ask them to perform some task for them that will "only take a second". This puts the individual in a bad position because they find it difficult to decline, and it also detracts from the priorities they have been tasked with by their leader. This adds stress to the individual and cuts into the ability of the overall team to produce. The request is seemingly harmless to the one asking it, and it actually might be if it were only one simple request on rare occasions. It becomes a problem when it starts to happen regularly and is something that you as the leader need to handle by communicating a process for requesting work from your team.

In many cases I found that when it came to priorities, many of the members of my team would feel like all of the balls they were juggling were glass, and when they would finally come to me for help, they would be completely stressed and buried under the weight of the priorities. In these cases, you have a few courses of action as a leader. The first thing to do is to understand all of the balls that person has in the air. Once you know the complete list of tasks, then you can identify for them the balls that are rubber and then put those aside for the time being. Make sure they understand how and why you decided that they were rubber so that they can increase their knowledge and confidence in making that decision in the future.

The next thing you can do is to take a look at any of the remaining glass balls and see if there is something you can do to help turn them into rubber balls. There were several times when I simply sent an email to a peer and respectfully asked if it would be okay if their request were completed the following week. In many cases it was just fine, and that glass ball just turned rubber. As a word of caution, don't forget to look at the rubber balls every now and then to make sure none of them have turned glass. In the following week the ball that I had turned rubber would be glass again and I couldn't turn it back without some cost.

Now what you have remaining is a smaller quantity of glass balls. If this quantity is acceptable, then you are done. If not, then you need to ask your team member to create for you the pros and cons of getting each one of these tasks complete, just like you did for your boss in our previous section. You may be able to help with this, but I typically preferred to have them tell me rather than me tell them. It was good experience for them as long as it was a relatively quick exercise with no formal presentation needed, just the information on a whiteboard or scratched on a piece of paper.

Once you have the information, then you and your team member can walk through it together. You can make decisions or allow them to, but in either case your decisions need to be communicated up and out. All affected parties, including your boss, need to know what is going on. Bear in mind your boss may veto your decision, and that's okay. I always found it helpful when I had to tell someone that something wasn't going to be completed on time to tell them what the plan was for getting it completed and when it would be, or, in the very least, tell them when I would be able to tell them. Most people are reasonable if they feel like you are being upfront with them and putting in an honest effort to do the best you can for them.

Managing priorities is definitely more art than science, but with some time and experience you can get better at managing the art of figuring them out and the value of definitive communication when things you are charged with delivering have to shift.

Notes

Decision Making

There were days in my career that I had to make so many decisions that I didn't even want to decide what to eat for dinner when I got home. Decision making is something that you will do all the time as a leader. People will be looking to you constantly to make decisions. You will deal with financial decisions, resource decisions, prioritization, personnel issues, promotions and raises, time management and a plethora of other things. Heck you might even have to decide whether to order pizza or sandwiches for your team on a Friday for lunch.

And everyone, both above and below you, will be looking to you to make the right decisions all of the time.

It can be stressful, exhausting, and rewarding all at the same time. This too, is something that gets easier with time and experience. You will make bad decisions at times, and those bad decisions will give you experience, and that experience will help you make better decisions in the future. And again, this is an area where you have to be willing to give yourself some grace when you make a bad decision. You're not alone. We've all had missteps, so don't be too hard on yourself when it happens.

I will start by saying that it is NEVER a good idea to make a business-related decision based on emotion. You need information to make a sound decision. Many times you will have imperfect or incomplete information, but will be forced to make a decision based on the information that you have. That's okay. It is not necessarily a wrong decision if you make it based on the information that you have at the time, even if new information becomes available that obviously impacts the correctness of the decision. If you wait for everything to be perfect, you will never be able to execute. Once you are comfortable that you have enough information to make a decently informed decision, then go ahead. Make the decision and document the criteria under which you made the decision. The world is constantly moving, and it's not going to stop so that you have everything you need to do everything perfectly. You have to be decisive and act, but also be able and willing to adapt as things change. If someone later on asks why you made a particular decision, you can show them the documentation and the sound reasoning behind making the decision with the information that was available at the time. This is a much better response to that question than having to say that you were mad because your pride was hurt, so you made that particular decision out of spite. One of these two answers will go over a lot better than the other.

When faced with a difficult decision, make sure you center yourself and focus on the good of the organization and the good of your team. For instance, you may need to make a decision about an individual on your team who produces very well, but is detrimental to the rest of your team, a "bad apple" as they say. The fact that they produce well is good for the organization. The fact that they bring down the productivity and morale of the rest of the team is bad for the team and ultimately might be worse for the organization than the productivity can offset. There are ways to manage through the situation, but ultimately you will have to decide to try to mend the culture of your team with this individual or let them go and sacrifice the productivity of that person. It is not always easy or clear what the right path is, but if you pay attention it may reveal itself.

Make sure you always know why you make the decisions you do. You don't have to document every single decision. That would be impossible. You should, however, always know why you made them because you will get asked and you will never know when or by whom. Be prepared to answer the question when and if it comes up.

I once had a boss who would sit in meetings and give ample opportunity for someone to make a decision on something, and if no one did, then he would. He was a fairly intimidating person, and I was young in my leadership career. While I was confident in my abilities, I was timid and wanted to make sure I was doing what the boss wanted. Even if I had an idea or a solution, I wouldn't speak up. That was my mistake. I would wait for my boss to tell me what to do, and then I would try to execute on what he wanted me to do. The problem was that I didn't know why he had made the decision that he did, and I was trying to execute on a decision that I didn't make and that he wouldn't remember.

There was one particular time when he and I were on a call with the CEO of one of our hospitals, and my boss asked me why I had made a particular decision. I hadn't made the decision, he had, but it was my responsibility, and it was my job. I couldn't defend the decision because I didn't know why he had made it. I looked like a complete idiot to the CEO, and my boss began to question my ability to perform my duties. I was embarrassed and infuriated. I remembered something another boss of mine had said once. He said, "I would rather get fired for doing what I think is right, than get fired for doing what someone else thinks is right." After I got over my emotions, I pulled myself up by the bootstraps and started doing my job.

I became more assertive and was not shy about presenting my ideas to my boss. He may have questioned them, but I always had a good reason for them, and he never rejected one of them. He was looking for me to step up, and I did. In a relatively short amount of time, I became his right-hand man, showing other leaders on his team how to operate well under him. It was a valuable lesson for me that I heeded for the rest of my career. I could defend any decision I made if I was asked.

Have confidence in yourself. Understand that you are in your position for a reason and believe in your own ability to lead and execute. Make your decisions based on the best information that you have available to you and always be able to explain why you decided the way you did. Do not be too proud to ask for help from your boss, your mentors, or even your peers. Their experience may be useful to you in making a better decision than you can on your own, but in the end, the decision is yours to make and to own. Don't be afraid of that.

Notes

Hiring

The single most important resource you have as a leader is your team. Hands down, without a doubt, if you do not have people to lead, then you are just a title in a suit. You are responsible for taking care of your team, for building the individuals, for their productivity, their mistakes, the culture, and even the attitude and feel of the team. It is all your responsibility, and your team will be a reflection of you as a leader. Do not take this lightly. It is an extremely important, if not the most important, part of being a leader. Every time you add or subtract a person from your team, you affect every aspect of the entire team.

Sometimes you do not have a choice as to who becomes part of your team. For instance, your extrinsic power may expand, and you could inherit an existing team and the individuals that come with it. In this case, it is very important for you to welcome these individuals and indoctrinate them into the culture of your team. This is a little more difficult than bringing in a new person or persons. Inherited team members may already have a developed culture that is different than the one on your team but has been their normal within the same organization. You have to be consistent in setting your expectations, give them time to unlearn their old ways, and relearn the way you want them to be a part of the culture of your team.

Other times you have the opportunity to bring in a new team member from outside of your team. My personal preference was to promote from within if at all possible. If I have a person on my team who I can promote into a more senior role and then bring in a new person to fill the role that the promoted team member vacated, then I prefer to do this. I would even bring on an interested member of another team before going outside the organization to fill a vacancy. Of course, this situation has to be handled appropriately with open communication. You do not want to be seen as a person who is soliciting other leaders' team members.

Promoting from within is typically a morale booster for the team in general. It is evidence that there is real opportunity for upward mobility for those who work hard and have the ambition to move up. It can be disheartening to team members who have worked hard and produced well to have someone from the outside hired in above them. Sometimes it is completely necessary, and it may lead to some tough conversations, but you can't promote someone into a position they are not ready for just so their feelings won't be hurt. You have to remember that your job is to add value to the organization and produce what they need you to produce. You are leading a team of professionals, not running a daycare. You may need to explain to an individual who did not get promoted the reasons why. In doing so, I found that it was helpful to outline the things that they could do to make themselves a viable candidate for the next time an opportunity for advancement presented itself.

When hiring from the outside to bring on a new team member, I would usually take the following steps in the process:

1. Tap into my own professional network
2. Take any recommendations from existing team members
3. Use internal recruiters (if available)
4. Use external recruiters

These activities can be happening simultaneously so you don't have to exhaust one avenue before going on to the next, unless you are not allowed to use external recruiters until the internal folks have a shot at filling a position.

It is good to use options one and two insomuch as there is a significant advantage to having a new team member who is not a completely unknown quantity. If someone recommends them or has worked with them before, and they would want to work with them again knowing the culture of the team they are on now, then orienting that new person becomes much easier. The risk of them having a negative impact on the team is greatly reduced, as well.

Human Resources is your friend. Use them for what they are in the organization for and allow them to add their value to the organization. Trying to go around them and do your own thing just causes headaches and makes things more difficult. Partner with them and cultivate the relationship. Your life will be much easier if you do. Let the internal recruiters do their job and help them by being as specific as you can about your needs. They may need some understanding of the skills you are looking for or help with some meaningful words or industry terms to help in their search. They can't be experts in every discipline, so do what you can to help them help you. I will say one thing about outside recruiters, they can be a valuable asset in the right situations, but I never accepted unsolicited resumes from an outside recruiter. This is a shady tactic and can lead to a battle over how a candidate got introduced to you. If they send a resume of someone who you end up hiring, then they may try to claim their fees even though you didn't ask for the resume. I've ended business relationships with more than one recruiter over behavior like this.

I will not go into the variety of interview methods and techniques, but I will say that there were a few things that I looked for in an interviewing candidate and why:

- A firm handshake and eye contact - confidence
- A hard copy of their resume – preparedness
- Taking notes when I spoke about the position, team, and company – attentive
- Ability to articulate their story succinctly – efficiency
- Answering questions I asked without fabricating answers – honesty

I realize that some of these are a bit outdated, e.g., a paper resume and taking notes, and I am not saying that these things need to be your criteria. I would, however, suggest that you spend some time thinking about the intangible things that are important to you in a team member and figuring out how to tease those out in an hour-long interview.

I very rarely would unilaterally hire a candidate. Obviously, it is not efficient to involve every person on the team in the interview process, but typically I would select two or three frontrunners, introduce them to the team, and get their input on them before making a decision. After all, they are the ones who are going to be working with them on a daily basis, and the new person will affect the energy on the team. The trick is to hire someone who will affect it in a positive way.

Don't get too hung up on resumes and credentials. On the other hand, you can't completely discount them, and there are certain positions that absolutely require adequate training or credentials. A college degree is a good thing, even if it is not in the discipline that you are hiring for. It shows commitment, follow through, and accomplishment. These are all good things. A learning point for me on this was the fact that one of the smartest people I ever met was a grocery store manager with a high school education who taught himself how to program. He became the president and CEO of a software company. I've also known Ivy Leaguers with MBA's who couldn't manage themselves out of a paper bag, let alone successfully lead a team.

Do not discount potential and ambition. A person may look like a rock star on paper, and maybe they are, but there's a reason they are looking for a job. They may not be a team player, or they may think that their skills and experience put them above others. I would rather have two good team members who work well together than two rocks stars who can produce individually, but can't work together. At the end of the day the "good" workers will outperform the rock stars and have a lot more fun doing it. If those "good" workers have ambition and potential, they will grow into rock stars in a short amount of time, and they will bring others along with them. This is invaluable to your team's culture and energy.

After many years of creating teams and interviewing hundreds of candidates, I can tell you two things that I learned:

1. It was very difficult for a candidate to change my mind after the first five minutes of an interview. You only have one chance to make a first impression.
2. Always trust your gut. Even if this person comes highly recommended, and their resume is 110% of what you are looking for, if your gut tells you not to, then don't. You will regret not listening to it.

Notes

Firing

The single most important resource you have as a leader is your team. Hands down, without a doubt, if you do not have people to lead, then you are just a title in a suit. You are responsible for taking care of your team, for building the individuals, for their productivity, their mistakes, the culture, and even the attitude and feel of the team. It is all your responsibility, and your team will be a reflection of you as a leader. Do not take this lightly. It is an extremely important, if not the most important, part of being a leader. Every time you add or subtract a person from your team, you affect every aspect of the entire team.

I know I just said that in the last chapter, but it is worth repeating. Just as adding a person changes the culture of a team, hopefully in a positive way, removing someone from the team changes it as well, again, hopefully in a positive way. Even if you remove a "bad apple" from the team, and it is the right thing to do for the team, the way you go about doing it can have a negative impact, so be careful not to instill a "fear of losing my job" in the rest of the team by not handling the removing of a "bad apple" in an appropriate way.

I truly believe that most people want to do a good job. As a leader, I always took it as my responsibility to put the right people in the right positions so that they could reach their fullest potential and add the most value to the organization. That being said, many times if I had a team member who was underperforming, I would give them chances to improve. This could be approached in several different ways, the simplest of which is to set clear and definitive expectations for that individual with very specific deliverables and timelines, as well as clearly communicated consequences for not meeting them.

Whenever I had these conversations, I would require that the team member send me an email with their understanding of what was expected of them and on what timeline. This would provide me with three things. First, I would be able to tell by what they wrote whether or not they understood the expectations. If their email did not adequately reflect what my expectations were, then I knew I needed to have a follow-up conversation to add clarity for them. Secondly, it would provide me with documentation that I could use later on if I needed to take further action. And thirdly, it would serve as a means for me to follow up on the conversation and progress. This is a key step.

If you set expectations and do not follow up on them, then you have effectively wasted your time, and the chances of the team member's performance improving is slim at best.

These are obviously not fun or comfortable conversations, but they are necessary at times. There were times during some of these conversations when an extenuating circumstance would be revealed to me that was a considerable factor in the lackluster performance. It could be a coworker, manager, or even a situation outside of work that was adding stress and affecting performance. If this was the case, then I would do my best to remedy the situation and allow the team member an opportunity to improve. We all have to work, and we all have other stresses in our life, too. On several occasions I had team members who just needed an hour or so once a week to take care of an elderly parent or to come in a little late one day to accommodate something for their children. Having them know that you understand that there are things in life that are more important than work can go a long way in relieving their stress about the situation and promoting loyalty at the same time. That's not to say that it is okay for their work to suffer and that not meeting expectations is acceptable. More often than not, if I allowed them the freedom to take care of the things that were important in their life, I was repaid tenfold in loyalty and productivity. When the chips were down and a deadline loomed, I knew they would step up and work very hard to deliver.

Occasionally, you may encounter a team member who does not gel with their immediate manager. In this situation you need to determine if you have a manager problem, a team member problem, or both. This is where you look at the proverbial bus. Ideally, you want each of your people on the right bus and in the right seat on the bus as Jim Collins so eloquently explains in his book *Good to Great.* If someone is not in the right seat, then what you need to do as a leader is to figure out what the right seat is. It may not be on your team, and that's okay. Remember, the point is to add value to the organization. If they can add more value on another team, then help them get into the right seat. The idea is the same for both a manager and an individual contributor. It's just a little more complex if you need do deal with the direct reports of a manager who is the one needing a new seat.

I would typically try a different seat on the bus for a person who was underperforming or just not reaching their potential in their current position. Many times, changing seats was effective and remedied the situation, but there were times when it was evident that the person was just on the wrong bus. It was not uncommon for me to actually help someone find a new position that was more suited to their skills and interests than the one they were in, whether it was inside or outside of the company we were both working for at the time.

When you hit the point when these corrective actions are not working, you may need to go down the path of firing a team member. I highly urge you to involve Human Resources from the beginning of the process. It works out better for everyone if you do. Share with them any documented conversations, expectations, timelines, etc. that you have from meeting with the individual. Follow HR's guidance on the steps and timelines required to remove an individual from your team. This may take several months and include steps such as verbal and written counseling, a formal performance plan, meetings with HR, and possibly multiple iterations of any part or the entire process. Be patient and follow the process. It can potentially salvage the team member, but in the very least, it protects the company in the long run.

When and if it comes time to actually have the conversation where you need to let a team member go, make sure you have someone else in the room with you, preferably an HR representative if possible. You do not want to get into a "he said, she said" situation. You need a witness. You will need to deliver the news clearly, succinctly, and unemotionally. It is not an easy thing to do, but this is not a discussion. If you are at the firing point, then the time for discussions has passed. The company may have policies on how the actual exit of the person must take place. If so, then follow them. If your company does not have them, then make sure there is no security risk with access to information or physical locations. Being fired can be a humiliating thing, so if you can, allow them to collect their belongings discreetly and exit with some dignity.

As I stated before, being able to take care of my team was something that was very important to me as a leader. Taking care of your team can take on many forms and entail many different activities, including having to remove someone from it. I always tried to do what was best for my team collectively and for the individuals on it. If I could avoid firing someone by finding something better for them or by relieving some stressor that allowed them to perform better, then I would do whatever I could to make that happen as long as it did not take away from the overall team or impact the value that the team was able to deliver to the organization. If attempted corrective action steps are ineffective in solving the problem, then it is your job as the leader to step up and protect the culture and productivity of your team by removing the source of the issues.

Notes

Conclusion

It seems a bit ironic to me to have a section on leadership entitled 'Conclusion' because there is no conclusion in leadership. It is an endless journey of learning and experiencing. There is not a definitive answer or formula that works in every situation. In my experience, the best leaders never stop learning. They always strive to be better, to seek new and better ways to add value, and to take care of their teams. It is my hope that what I have written in this short book will be of assistance to you on your leadership journey, that it will help you avoid some of the mistakes I made on mine, and that it will help you to become a better leader than I ever was. Best of Luck to you!

The Fitzgerald Freedom Ranch is a 114 acre property in Mt. Pleasant, TN that exists to help veterans recalibrate, re-engage in civilian society and be able to experience the joy of life that so many of them have lost. Proceeds from the Homegrown Leadership program will go directly to support the property and intentions of the ranch.